# HOW SPACE MANUFACTURING WILL CHANGE EVERYTHING
## New Frontier of Innovation

*Why Microgravity Engineering Could Be the Key to a Revolutionary Future*

Tommy S. Manley

Copyright ©Tommy S. Manley, 2024.

All rights reserved. No part of this publication may be reproduced, distributed, or transmitted in any form or by any means, including photocopying, recording, or other electronic or mechanical methods, without the prior written permission of the publisher, except in the case of brief quotations embodied in critical reviews and certain other noncommercial uses permitted by copyright law.

# Table of Contents

Introduction ........................................................................... 4
Chapter 1: The Vision for Space Manufacturing ....... 8
Chapter 2: Why Microgravity Changes the Game ... 18
Chapter 3: Cutting-Edge Applications of Space Manufacturing ................................................................. 29
Chapter 4: Breakthroughs in Medicine from Space Manufacturing ................................................................. 39
Chapter 5: Communication and Data Revolution Through Space-Produced Fiber Optics .................... 49
Chapter 6: Building Infrastructure in Space with 3D Printing ............................................................................ 58
Chapter 7: Overcoming Challenges in Space Manufacturing ................................................................. 69
Chapter 8: Environmental and Ethical Considerations ................................................................ 81
Chapter 9: The Future of Space Manufacturing ...... 92
Conclusion ...................................................................... 105

# Introduction

Space manufacturing, an emerging frontier in human innovation, is not just a concept of science fiction—it's an active pursuit reshaping our understanding of industry, technology, and economic potential. At its core, space manufacturing revolves around producing goods in the unique conditions found beyond Earth's atmosphere, particularly in microgravity. Unlike the pull of Earth's gravity, microgravity allows for the creation of materials and structures in ways that are impossible down here. When gravity's influence is minimized, the dynamics of how particles interact, bond, and solidify change, unlocking possibilities for manufacturing that are groundbreaking, including the potential for perfectly structured fiber optics, complex medical bioprinting, and the assembly of large-scale structures in orbit.

The journey toward making space an industrial playground didn't happen overnight. In the latter half of the 20th century, space exploration was primarily driven by national pride and scientific discovery. But as time progressed, the value of space exploration as a commercial opportunity became evident. NASA pioneered the groundwork for human spaceflight and technological research, paving the way for advancements we rely on every day, from satellite communications to GPS. The Apollo missions, as iconic as they were for bringing humanity to the Moon, also set a precedent for ambitious endeavors in space, laying the seeds for what would eventually grow into commercial interest.

Fast forward to today, and space is no longer the exclusive domain of government agencies. Private companies like Blue Origin, Boeing, and SpaceX are not just dreaming about space; they're actively transforming it into an operational field for science and industry. Blue Origin, for example, envisions a sustainable human presence in space, looking toward a future where industries can thrive off-planet. Boeing, with its rich aerospace legacy, is collaborating on projects like Orbital Reef, a commercial space station that could one day host researchers, scientists, and even tourists, all in the name of advancing space-based industry. SpaceX, known for its impressive strides in rocket reusability, has made space travel more affordable and accessible, allowing more companies and researchers to consider the practicalities of conducting experiments and manufacturing in orbit.

This shift toward commercial involvement is not merely about profits; it's about expanding humanity's capability to innovate in ways that benefit life on Earth. Space manufacturing presents new opportunities to produce materials and conduct experiments that Earth's gravity would complicate or even prevent. Fiber optic cables made in space, for example, can achieve unprecedented clarity and efficiency, benefiting global communication infrastructure. Meanwhile, bioprinting human tissues in microgravity could revolutionize regenerative medicine, offering potential treatments and replacements for damaged organs without the complications faced in Earth's environment.

The purpose of this book is to explore the transformative potential of space manufacturing, bridging the technical concepts with real-world implications in a way that captures the imagination and reveals the tangible impact this new frontier could have on daily life. As humanity stands at the cusp of its next great industrial leap, the insights here aim to illustrate how manufacturing in space could lead to innovations that reshape technology, healthcare, infrastructure, and the global economy. This topic isn't just about distant possibilities; it's about a rapidly approaching reality that holds revolutionary promise.

# Chapter 1: The Vision for Space Manufacturing

The concept of space as a site for manufacturing and research may sound futuristic, yet its roots trace back to the earliest space missions. When humanity first reached beyond Earth's atmosphere, the main focus was on exploration—sending astronauts and probes to uncover the mysteries of space. But as missions progressed, scientists noticed that the weightless environment of microgravity could unlock unique conditions for experimentation, prompting a new line of thought: what if this environment could be harnessed not just for exploration, but for creating things that couldn't be made on Earth? The seeds for space manufacturing were planted, though it would take decades for them to start bearing fruit.

In the 1970s, NASA's Skylab mission offered a glimpse into how materials and biological studies could behave in space. Skylab was not just America's first space station but also a floating laboratory, where astronauts conducted experiments in microgravity, observing how materials and fluids behaved without Earth's pull. This provided early insights into the effects of weightlessness on processes like crystal growth and fluid dynamics. The International Space Station (ISS), launched in 1998 as a joint effort among NASA, Roscosmos, ESA, and other international space agencies, took this concept further. Its laboratories became home to more complex experiments, including early tests in bioprinting, materials science, and even small-scale manufacturing—each of these experiments contributing to the foundation of what we now call space manufacturing.

Today, this foundation is being built upon by private companies that are transforming the idea of space-based industry from an abstract possibility to a concrete goal. Blue Origin, for instance, has set its sights on making space a place where people can live, work, and innovate. Founded by Jeff Bezos,

Blue Origin's ambition goes beyond launching rockets; it envisions a future where industrial operations can move off-planet, preserving Earth's resources and ecosystem. Their proposed *Orbital Reef* is designed as a multi-use space station that could host research labs, manufacturing facilities, and even space tourism, providing a commercialized approach to space habitation that encourages industry to thrive in orbit.

Boeing, a titan in aerospace engineering, has leveraged its extensive experience to contribute to this vision. Boeing's involvement with NASA's ISS and its proposed participation in Orbital Reef align with its commitment to making space an accessible and sustainable environment for research and production. Through its work on the Starliner capsule and partnerships with NASA, Boeing has consistently pushed for advancements that enable human presence in space. As a result, the company is positioned to help lead the charge in establishing the necessary infrastructure to support industries that could one day operate entirely in microgravity.

Redwire, another key player, focuses specifically on space-based manufacturing and infrastructure. Founded with a mission to expand the industrial possibilities of space, Redwire has been pioneering projects that push the boundaries of what's feasible in a microgravity environment. Its *Archinaut One* satellite, for example, combines 3D printing with robotic assembly, allowing for the in-orbit construction of large structures. This capability could revolutionize satellite deployment, making it possible to build larger, more complex satellites directly in space without the size and weight limitations imposed by Earth's gravity. By minimizing the constraints of traditional manufacturing and construction methods, Redwire's contributions are paving the way for a new era where entire infrastructures can be assembled in orbit.

These companies represent just the beginning of what could become a bustling industrial sector beyond Earth's atmosphere. Their innovations are driven by a shared belief that microgravity holds untapped potential for creating materials, devices, and even biological constructs that Earth-bound conditions simply can't replicate. Through their efforts, the idea of space manufacturing has evolved from a speculative thought into a goal within reach, and their work continues to lay the groundwork for future generations to explore, produce, and sustain life beyond our home planet.

Orbital Reef, one of the most ambitious projects in modern space exploration, represents a transformative leap in how we envision the purpose of a space station. Designed by Blue Origin and Boeing, it aims to be the world's first commercially operated space station, providing a platform for diverse activities ranging from scientific research to manufacturing, and even potential tourism. While traditional space stations like the ISS are primarily government-funded and dedicated to scientific research, Orbital Reef shifts the focus toward creating an accessible, multi-use facility that encourages private companies, researchers, and even non-government organizations to utilize space for their own ventures. This station could serve as a hub for manufacturing high-value products in microgravity, allowing for innovations in materials science, bioprinting, and more—paving the way for industries that can't thrive on Earth.

Orbital Reef is conceptualized as a "mixed-use business park" in low Earth orbit, with modular facilities that can be customized for various purposes. The vision extends beyond merely renting out space for research; it's about creating an environment where multiple industries can collaborate, innovate, and produce. With dedicated sections for life sciences, engineering labs, and commercial production, Orbital Reef is designed to be adaptable, growing as demand increases and accommodating activities that range from high-stakes research to tourism. This marks a shift in the way we think about space infrastructure, moving from government-led projects to a more inclusive, commercially viable space ecosystem.

However, such a bold vision does not come without its challenges. The concept of a commercially operated space station requires overcoming several technical and economic barriers. Building and maintaining a space station is an enormously expensive undertaking, and unlike government-funded stations, Orbital Reef must attract consistent commercial interest to remain viable. The upfront costs alone are staggering; everything from developing the station's technology to launching the necessary materials and modules into space demands extensive investment. Moreover, operating in low Earth orbit exposes the station to extreme conditions, such as radiation and temperature fluctuations, which require advanced materials and protective measures to ensure safety and longevity.

Public skepticism is another hurdle. As enticing as a commercial space station sounds, questions arise about its real-world feasibility. Critics argue that, while Orbital Reef may appeal to a select group of high-profile companies, it's uncertain whether there will be sustained interest from enough commercial tenants to justify the costs. Some question whether the promised uses—such as manufacturing fiber optics or conducting medical research in microgravity—can generate sufficient demand to offset the station's high operating costs. Additionally, the idea of space tourism, while increasingly popular, faces its own set of challenges. The high cost of space travel remains prohibitive for most people, limiting the potential customer base to a wealthy few, which raises concerns about the long-term economic model.

Another layer of complexity lies in the technical demands of constructing and maintaining a fully functional habitat in space. Orbital Reef's designers must address not only the need for life support systems, energy generation, and radiation shielding but also the logistical challenges of transporting supplies and equipment. Even the most routine maintenance tasks become more complicated in microgravity, requiring specialized equipment and training for the station's inhabitants. Furthermore, any facility in low Earth orbit is vulnerable to debris, which poses a constant threat to its structure and safety. Engineers must design Orbital Reef with these risks in mind, incorporating fail-safes, redundancies, and advanced shielding to mitigate the dangers of collisions with space debris.

Despite these obstacles, Orbital Reef represents a daring and visionary step forward. If successful, it could not only pave the way for sustainable space industry but also shift humanity's relationship with space from one of exploration to one of habitation and utilization. Achieving this vision requires not only cutting-edge technology but also a paradigm shift in how society views space: not just as a scientific frontier, but as a place where people and businesses can work, live, and create. While the hurdles are significant, the potential rewards are transformative, promising an era where space is no longer the final frontier but an integrated part of human enterprise and innovation.

## Chapter 2: Why Microgravity Changes the Game

Microgravity, the condition of near-weightlessness experienced in space, brings a set of unique properties that alter the fundamental behaviors of materials, fluids, and biological processes. Unlike on Earth, where gravity constantly pulls matter downward, microgravity allows particles, liquids, and gases to float and interact more freely, creating conditions that open up entirely new possibilities for manufacturing, research, and even medicine. In this environment, materials and biological tissues can be formed in ways that gravity would otherwise disrupt, offering a host of advantages for producing high-value products.

One of the most transformative aspects of microgravity is its impact on materials science. On Earth, gravity often leads to sedimentation and convection in molten materials, creating imperfections as materials cool and solidify. In space, however, these effects are minimized, allowing materials to form with fewer structural defects and greater uniformity. Take, for instance, ZBLAN fiber optics—a type of high-grade glass fiber. When produced on Earth, these fibers often crystallize as they cool, leading to imperfections that limit their efficiency for data transmission. In microgravity, ZBLAN fibers can be produced without these flaws, creating an ultra-clear material that significantly reduces signal loss over long distances. This improvement holds the potential to revolutionize telecommunications infrastructure, as it could enable faster, more reliable data transmission across vast distances with fewer signal boosters.

Biological processes also respond dramatically to microgravity. Cells and tissues grow differently when freed from Earth's gravitational pull, which has exciting implications for fields like bioprinting and regenerative medicine. On Earth, printing complex biological tissues is challenging because gravity affects the layering process, causing soft tissues to collapse before they're fully formed. In microgravity, however, cells can hold their structure longer, enabling the possibility of printing tissues and organs with more accuracy and stability. Experiments conducted on the International Space Station (ISS) have already shown promising results, with scientists successfully printing heart-like tissue and cartilage in space. These breakthroughs suggest that in the future, we may be able to produce entire organs in orbit, potentially revolutionizing transplantation and reducing the need for organ donors on Earth.

The absence of gravity's pull also impacts fluids and their behavior in surprising ways. In space, liquids naturally form into spheres due to surface tension, which allows researchers to experiment with fluid dynamics in ways that would be impossible on Earth. For manufacturing, this means the ability to mix and create materials with greater precision, as microgravity eliminates the stratification that often occurs when fluids with different densities are combined. This property is especially advantageous for creating pharmaceuticals and high-performance alloys, where even minor imperfections can impact the product's effectiveness or strength.

From an economic standpoint, microgravity offers clear advantages for producing high-value products that can justify the costs of space manufacturing. The materials produced in space, like flawless fiber optics and complex biological tissues, have significant commercial value due to their superior quality and performance. As space infrastructure improves and the costs of transporting goods and materials decrease, producing these high-value items in orbit could become economically viable. The potential profit margins from selling these products on Earth could help offset the initial costs, making space manufacturing a sustainable business model.

Technologically, microgravity creates a new frontier where scientific principles can be tested and applied in innovative ways. Engineers and scientists have a blank canvas in space, free from the physical constraints imposed by Earth's gravity. This environment allows for the creation of advanced materials with higher strength, greater purity, and lower residual stress. For instance, metal alloys and ceramics produced in space could be engineered for extreme durability, opening up possibilities for applications in aerospace, defense, and advanced electronics. Moreover, the freedom from gravity's limitations enables the construction of larger and more intricate structures, such as satellites and solar panels, that can be assembled directly in orbit without the size constraints required for Earth-based launch.

In essence, the unique properties of microgravity are paving the way for innovations that were once the realm of science fiction. By harnessing the benefits of near-weightlessness, space manufacturing offers a gateway to products and technologies with unprecedented quality and complexity. These advantages make microgravity not just a scientific curiosity but a powerful catalyst for the next industrial revolution—one that might redefine everything from medicine and telecommunications to material science and global infrastructure.

The contrasts between production on Earth and in space stem fundamentally from gravity's pervasive influence. On Earth, gravity dictates how materials settle, mix, and bond, often creating imperfections that limit the structural and functional qualities of manufactured goods. In the near-weightless environment of space, these gravitational forces are almost nonexistent, allowing for entirely different production processes that yield products of higher purity, consistency, and, in many cases, enhanced performance. This distinction forms the basis of a burgeoning industry, as microgravity is proving to be a powerful enabler of innovation in fields ranging from materials science to medicine.

One of the most illustrative examples of this difference is in the production of ZBLAN fiber optics. ZBLAN, a fluoride-based glass, holds promise as a highly efficient material for fiber-optic cables due to its potential for ultra-low signal loss. On Earth, when ZBLAN is drawn into fibers, gravity induces crystallization as the material cools, creating microscopic imperfections that scatter light and reduce efficiency. This limitation means that data signals sent through ZBLAN fibers lose quality over relatively short distances, necessitating signal boosters. In the microgravity of space, however, ZBLAN fibers can cool without these crystallization issues, resulting in ultra-clear, defect-free fibers that vastly outperform their Earth-made counterparts. By reducing signal loss over long distances, space-produced ZBLAN could revolutionize global communications, providing faster, more reliable internet across continents and oceans.

Another area where space production shines is in the realm of bioprinting. On Earth, printing tissues and organs is a complex process due to gravity's effect on soft biological materials, which often collapse under their own weight before they can be fully structured. In microgravity, cells and biomaterials can be layered more precisely and retain their shapes longer, allowing for the possibility of producing viable tissues with intricate structures. Experiments aboard the ISS have demonstrated that tissues, such as cartilage and heart-like constructs, can be successfully printed in space, setting the stage for more advanced biological manufacturing. If scaled, this technology could provide on-demand organs for transplants, bypassing the issues of organ rejection and shortages on Earth.

Microgravity's influence extends to metal and alloy production as well. On Earth, molten metals are affected by gravity-induced convection and sedimentation, leading to inconsistencies in structure. Space production eliminates these variables, enabling metals to form with a more uniform molecular structure. This quality is essential for high-performance alloys used in aerospace and electronics, where structural integrity is paramount. A metal component manufactured in microgravity could exhibit higher strength, lower residual stress, and enhanced resistance to wear and tear compared to one produced on Earth.

Microgravity is not merely a tool for improving existing processes; it also serves as a catalyst for breakthroughs that are otherwise unattainable on Earth. In the absence of gravity, scientists can observe and manipulate fundamental physical and biological processes with unparalleled clarity. This unique environment is driving innovations that push the boundaries of what's possible in manufacturing and research.

For example, pharmaceutical research benefits immensely from microgravity. Certain drugs and proteins crystallize more uniformly in space, allowing researchers to study their structures with greater accuracy. This structural insight can lead to the development of more effective drugs, particularly in treating complex diseases like cancer and Alzheimer's. In fact, some companies are already conducting experiments on the ISS to produce drugs with enhanced efficacy, leveraging the clarity provided by space-grown protein crystals.

Beyond improving specific materials or products, the unique conditions of space manufacturing are reshaping how we approach large-scale construction. Traditional satellites and space structures are limited by the size and shape of rockets, as they must fit into a narrow payload fairing. However, with 3D printing and robotic assembly in space, satellites and other structures can be built directly in orbit, circumventing these size constraints. Projects like Redwire's Archinaut One are pioneering this approach, allowing for the construction of expansive solar arrays and other structures that would be infeasible to launch as a single piece from Earth. These technologies could one day enable the assembly of space habitats or massive power-generating stations, laying the groundwork for future space colonies and advanced infrastructure in orbit.

In essence, the absence of gravity creates an environment where conventional limits no longer apply. Microgravity is driving innovation by revealing new properties in materials, enabling advanced medical research, and facilitating large-scale construction. As humanity looks to solve complex problems on Earth, space production provides an extraordinary toolkit for pioneering solutions, transforming the limitations of our home planet into the possibilities of a universe-wide industrial landscape. Through space manufacturing, we're not just enhancing products; we're rethinking the very processes of production and discovery, propelling industries into an era of unprecedented advancement.

# Chapter 3: Cutting-Edge Applications of Space Manufacturing

Bioprinting and tissue engineering, promising fields within regenerative medicine, are reaching unprecedented heights in space, thanks to the microgravity environment. On Earth, creating complex, layered structures like tissues and organs poses challenges, particularly because biological materials are soft and prone to collapse under gravity. This limitation has historically made it difficult to print fully functional organs or intricate tissues that can retain their shape long enough to develop and mature. In space, however, the lack of gravitational force allows scientists to create biological structures that can hold together more naturally, encouraging advancements that could transform the future of healthcare.

Microgravity provides a unique setting where cells can be layered in three dimensions without succumbing to gravitational pressure. This stability enables researchers to print complex tissues with more precision and intricacy than is possible on Earth. For instance, experiments conducted on the International Space Station (ISS) have successfully produced cartilage and heart-like tissues, which retain their structure and function more effectively than on Earth. These early successes open the door to creating more complex organs, potentially including kidneys, livers, and even lungs, in the future. The long-term goal is to make it possible for organs to be printed directly in space, then transported to Earth for transplantation, bypassing the complications of organ shortages and immune rejection associated with traditional transplants.

The bioprinting of tissues in space is also shedding light on fundamental cell behaviors, which are crucial to understanding diseases and developing treatments. By observing how cells differentiate and organize themselves in a weightless environment, scientists can gain valuable insights into cell growth and regeneration. This knowledge could lead to breakthroughs in regenerative medicine on Earth, improving the way doctors approach conditions that require tissue repair or replacement.

In addition to the strides in bioprinting, the production of advanced materials in microgravity is paving the way for transformative infrastructure innovations. ZBLAN fiber optics are a prime example of how space production can yield superior materials that meet the demands of modern telecommunications. ZBLAN, a fluoride-based glass, possesses properties that make it ideal for fiber optics due to its potential to reduce signal loss to a fraction of what's currently achievable with silica-based fibers. However, producing ZBLAN fibers on Earth is challenging; during the cooling process, gravity-induced crystallization often leads to imperfections that limit the fiber's optical clarity. These flaws disrupt the transmission of data, creating signal loss that accumulates over long distances.

In space, however, ZBLAN fibers can be manufactured without the crystallization issues caused by gravity, resulting in ultra-clear, defect-free fibers. This clarity means that ZBLAN fiber optics can transmit data over thousands of miles with minimal signal loss, greatly surpassing the performance of traditional fiber optics. For the telecommunications industry, this improvement is monumental. By using ZBLAN in undersea cables, for example, data could flow across continents without the need for numerous signal boosters, leading to faster and more efficient global communications. The economic potential of ZBLAN fibers is substantial, as they could enable the next generation of high-speed internet and data services, bridging gaps in connectivity for remote or underserved regions.

Both bioprinting and ZBLAN fiber production illustrate how microgravity is enabling advancements that go beyond incremental improvements. Instead, it's opening doors to technologies that can reshape entire industries. In bioprinting, the prospect of developing organs and complex tissues in space could redefine how we approach transplants and regenerative medicine, potentially saving countless lives. Meanwhile, the production of ZBLAN fiber optics could revolutionize data infrastructure, providing a new level of clarity and efficiency that Earth-based manufacturing simply cannot achieve. These innovations underscore how space is becoming a crucial laboratory for progress, where the absence of gravity allows for breakthroughs that have lasting impacts back on Earth. Through space manufacturing, we are not only expanding our technological capabilities but also enhancing our quality of life, setting the stage for a future where the limits of gravity no longer hold us back.

The concept of 3D printing in space represents a pivotal shift in how we think about manufacturing, allowing materials and tools to be created on-demand, directly in orbit. Since 2014, the International Space Station (ISS) has served as a testbed for 3D printing experiments, giving researchers invaluable insight into how materials behave in microgravity. By enabling the creation of parts and tools in space, 3D printing reduces the need for resupply missions, lowers costs, and supports longer-duration missions. The ISS's early experiments demonstrated that items such as small tools and machine parts could be printed in microgravity, showing promise for a future where spacecraft and stations are increasingly self-sufficient.

Beyond basic items, researchers are now exploring the potential for printing more complex and specialized materials, such as metals, ceramics, and advanced composites. On Earth, manufacturing high-performance materials often requires carefully controlled conditions to avoid defects and stresses. In microgravity, however, materials can solidify more evenly, creating a homogeneous structure with fewer imperfections. This quality is particularly advantageous for metals and ceramics, which can be printed with greater strength and durability than their Earth-made counterparts. For instance, heat-resistant ceramics printed in space could be used in extreme conditions, such as for rocket engines or high-temperature shielding. Additionally, composites and metal alloys created in space could offer unique structural benefits, leading to lighter, stronger materials ideal for aerospace and defense applications.

The future of 3D printing in space doesn't stop at small tools or specialized materials. Scientists and engineers are looking toward creating entire infrastructure elements, such as satellites, solar arrays, and structural components for space habitats, directly in orbit. This ambition is driving projects like Archinaut One, an initiative by Redwire that combines 3D printing with robotic assembly to construct and deploy large-scale structures in space. Archinaut One represents a breakthrough in self-assembling technology, with the capability to print and assemble components autonomously, without the limitations imposed by traditional rocket payload sizes.

One of the biggest constraints in launching satellites and large structures is the size and shape of rocket fairings. Every satellite or component must be compact enough to fit within a rocket's payload, leading to complex and costly engineering solutions. With Archinaut One's ability to construct and deploy structures directly in orbit, the limitations of Earth-based launch dimensions are no longer an issue. This enables engineers to design larger, more efficient satellites and infrastructure without folding mechanisms or other design compromises.

The Archinaut One project specifically aims to build solar arrays for satellites in space, allowing even small satellites to deploy expansive, power-generating surfaces that would otherwise be impractical to launch from Earth. By constructing these arrays in orbit, satellites can generate more power than would be possible with Earth-launched configurations, enhancing their operational capabilities and extending their lifespans. Looking further ahead, the ability to print and assemble structures in space opens up possibilities for vast infrastructure, including large solar power stations, research facilities, and even habitats for human occupancy.

The integration of 3D printing with autonomous assembly represents a leap forward in creating sustainable space-based infrastructure. Imagine, for instance, the potential for building a large-scale solar power station in orbit, capable of capturing sunlight continuously without atmospheric interference and transmitting that energy to Earth. This type of infrastructure would be a massive step toward sustainable energy production and a critical support for more ambitious space missions in the future.

Together, 3D printing and self-assembling technology are laying the groundwork for a future where space-based construction is not only feasible but essential. As the need for infrastructure in space grows, these technologies could revolutionize how we approach satellite design, space habitats, and energy generation. They also reduce the dependency on Earth-based resupply, supporting the long-term vision of a space economy where resources are produced, maintained, and repaired in orbit. This convergence of innovation marks the beginning of a new era, where humanity can start building its presence in space on an unprecedented scale. Through advancements like 3D printing and projects like Archinaut One, we are taking the first steps toward a space infrastructure that is resilient, adaptable, and capable of supporting the ambitious goals of tomorrow.

# Chapter 4: Breakthroughs in Medicine from Space Manufacturing

Bioprinting human tissues and organs in the microgravity environment of space offers transformative possibilities for medicine, with potential applications that go far beyond what is achievable on Earth. On the ground, gravity imposes significant limitations on the precision and structural integrity of bioprinted tissues. Soft biological materials, such as cells and scaffolding used in bioprinting, struggle to maintain their shape and form under gravity's constant pull, often resulting in deformation or collapse before the structure can stabilize. In space, however, the absence of this gravitational force enables cells to be layered in complex, three-dimensional arrangements that hold together naturally, providing scientists with a unique opportunity to explore more sophisticated tissue structures.

In microgravity, bioprinting becomes not just easier but also opens up avenues for creating more functional and complex biological constructs. Early experiments on the International Space Station (ISS) have already demonstrated that heart-like tissues and cartilage can be printed in space with a level of precision and durability that's difficult to replicate on Earth. The implications for regenerative medicine are profound: by harnessing microgravity, researchers could eventually bioprint entire organs, such as kidneys or livers, that function as seamlessly as natural organs. This could help address the critical shortage of transplantable organs, offering new hope to patients awaiting life-saving procedures and reducing the complications of immune rejection, as these bioprinted organs could be tailored to the patient's own cells.

Beyond structural advantages, microgravity also has a direct impact on cell growth and differentiation, which is crucial in regenerative medicine. Studies have shown that cells in microgravity behave differently, often exhibiting unique growth patterns that can improve the quality of tissue engineering. In space, cells tend to grow more symmetrically and form tighter, more cohesive clusters. This natural behavior enables the formation of tissues that are more structurally and functionally similar to those in the human body. For example, scientists have observed that certain stem cells can proliferate more rapidly and with greater differentiation potential in microgravity, accelerating the process of creating specialized cells necessary for tissue repair and regeneration.

These cellular dynamics in microgravity pave the way for advanced regenerative therapies that could revolutionize how we treat a variety of conditions. In particular, the ability to grow bone, cartilage, and even neural tissues in space could lead to breakthroughs in repairing damage from injuries or degenerative diseases. Consider, for instance, the potential to regenerate damaged cartilage for individuals suffering from joint disorders, or to grow neural tissue that could assist in the treatment of neurodegenerative conditions. The insights gained from these space-based experiments are already guiding new strategies for regenerative medicine on Earth, as researchers learn more about how cells organize and function in a gravity-free environment.

The microgravity environment also holds promise for complex surgical applications, where printed tissues could be produced in space and sent back to Earth for use in patients. With further advancements, the idea of space-produced organs could become a reality, leading to a scenario where hospitals could receive bioprinted organs from orbital facilities, circumventing Earth's limitations and time constraints in organ production. This would not only increase the availability of organs but also allow for customizable, patient-specific organs that reduce the risk of immune rejection and the need for long-term immunosuppressive therapy.

In addition to the direct benefits for tissue engineering and organ production, the insights gained from microgravity-based bioprinting are contributing valuable data to the field of cellular biology. By studying how cells behave in microgravity, scientists are uncovering new information about cellular processes, tissue development, and disease mechanisms. This research is already impacting drug development and disease modeling, allowing pharmaceutical companies to test drug effects on 3D cell cultures that more accurately reflect human tissue than conventional 2D cultures. As a result, new treatments could be developed faster, with a higher degree of effectiveness and fewer side effects.

In essence, microgravity offers a fertile ground for advancements in bioprinting and regenerative medicine, transforming the possibilities for human health. As research continues, the dream of creating patient-specific organs in space, repairing damaged tissues with precision, and understanding cell behavior on a deeper level could soon move from experimental stages to practical applications. The integration of space and medicine is showing us a future where human biology and technology work together seamlessly, enabling breakthroughs that could redefine how we understand and treat the human body. Through the bioprinting of tissues and organs, we are not just pushing the boundaries of medical science; we are creating the foundations of a new era in healthcare, where space itself becomes a resource for healing and renewal.

In the realm of medical advancements, space offers a unique environment where certain processes, difficult or even impossible on Earth, become far more feasible. The absence of gravity in space allows scientists to explore new ways of growing, preserving, and even enhancing biological materials, particularly in fields like organ preservation and stem cell research. Here, microgravity becomes an invaluable tool, reducing constraints that Earth's gravity imposes on these delicate and complex processes.

One of the greatest challenges in medicine today is organ preservation. Organs destined for transplant have a limited window of viability outside the body, typically measured in hours. On Earth, this limitation is due in part to the damage that can occur as organs are stored and transported under the effects of gravity. Fluids within organs can settle unevenly, leading to cellular stress and degradation. Microgravity, however, changes the game. Without gravity pulling fluids downward, tissues can remain more uniformly hydrated, reducing the cellular stress and minimizing the risk of ischemic injury—the damage caused by insufficient blood supply. In microgravity, organs could potentially be stored for longer periods, opening new avenues for transporting organs across greater distances and expanding the reach of life-saving transplant procedures.

Stem cell research also stands to benefit immensely from the microgravity environment of space. Stem cells have remarkable regenerative properties, but growing them consistently on Earth presents difficulties. Gravity affects how cells grow and differentiate, often causing stem cells to settle and clump unevenly. In space, stem cells can grow in three dimensions with less restriction, promoting a more natural and uniform development. Studies conducted on the International Space Station have shown that stem cells exhibit accelerated growth and higher differentiation potential in microgravity, which can yield a larger number of high-quality stem cells suitable for therapeutic applications. This discovery is particularly promising for regenerative medicine, as it allows for the generation of cells that can be used to treat a range of conditions, from tissue damage to degenerative diseases.

The potential for improved stem cell growth in space is especially valuable for developing treatments for conditions that require cellular regeneration, such as spinal cord injuries, heart disease, and neurological disorders. By producing stem cells in orbit, scientists could secure a more reliable supply of regenerative cells with enhanced qualities, expediting treatment development and enabling new therapies that could change the landscape of medical care on Earth. Furthermore, the insights gained from observing how stem cells behave in space could inform better techniques for cultivating these cells on Earth, bridging the gap between experimental research and clinical application.

Additionally, the ability to conduct experiments on cellular aging and disease modeling in space provides invaluable data for understanding how cells respond to stress and repair themselves. Space-based research into how cells age and respond to damage without gravity could help scientists uncover the mechanisms behind cellular degradation, leading to breakthroughs in treatments for age-related diseases. By studying these processes in a gravity-free environment, scientists can observe cellular reactions more clearly and develop new ways to preserve and repair cells, contributing to treatments that could extend organ health and longevity.

In summary, the conditions of space offer unparalleled opportunities for overcoming Earth-based limitations in medical science. Microgravity provides an environment where organs can be preserved more effectively, stem cells can grow with greater uniformity, and cellular behaviors can be studied without gravitational interference. As research in these areas progresses, the applications could transform not only how we approach transplants and regenerative therapies but also how we understand and combat diseases linked to cellular degradation. Through space-based medical advancements, we are pushing past the boundaries of what's possible on Earth, enabling new solutions that have the potential to enhance and extend human health in unprecedented ways.

# Chapter 5: Communication and Data Revolution Through Space-Produced Fiber Optics

ZBLAN fiber optics represent a significant leap forward in the field of data transmission, offering properties that traditional silica-based fibers simply cannot match. Composed of a fluoride-based glass material, ZBLAN possesses an inherent ability to transmit data with drastically lower signal loss, making it an ideal candidate for applications requiring high efficiency over long distances. The challenge, however, lies in manufacturing it with the clarity and uniformity needed to achieve its full potential. On Earth, gravity interferes with the cooling process of ZBLAN, leading to crystallization within the fiber structure. These crystallizations create imperfections that scatter light and diminish signal quality. As a result, silica fiber, though less efficient, remains the standard due to the production difficulties with ZBLAN.

In the microgravity environment of space, however, the manufacturing of ZBLAN fibers is transformed. Without the influence of gravity, ZBLAN fibers can cool evenly, avoiding the crystallization that occurs on Earth. This results in fibers with fewer impurities and a more homogenous structure, allowing for a transmission quality far superior to any Earth-made counterpart. Tests on the International Space Station have shown that ZBLAN produced in microgravity demonstrates exceptional optical clarity, with the potential to carry signals over distances of up to 2,000 kilometers before experiencing the same level of signal loss that silica fibers encounter over just 10 kilometers. This efficiency not only improves data quality but also reduces the need for signal-boosting repeaters, which are both costly and energy-intensive to install and maintain.

The implications of ZBLAN fibers for data transmission are profound. In undersea cables that link continents, for example, ZBLAN could enable faster and more reliable communication, eliminating many of the challenges associated with current fiber optic technology. Traditional fiber networks require frequent signal repeaters across oceanic distances to maintain data integrity. ZBLAN's low-loss transmission could reduce or even eliminate these repeaters, making data networks more resilient and lowering the overall cost of maintenance. Additionally, by reducing interruptions in signal flow, ZBLAN could offer lower latency for high-speed internet connections, directly impacting global communication and business operations.

Beyond undersea cables, ZBLAN could also revolutionize other areas of the global data infrastructure. As data demands grow exponentially, with applications ranging from cloud computing to real-time data analytics, the need for faster and more reliable networks becomes increasingly pressing. ZBLAN's ability to support high-capacity data streams over long distances would enhance data centers, telecommunications networks, and satellite communications, offering an efficient alternative to current fiber optics. For instance, rural and remote regions that rely on long-distance connections would benefit from improved network stability and faster internet speeds, helping bridge the digital divide by making advanced communications technology more accessible.

ZBLAN fiber optics, produced in the unique environment of space, could represent the next frontier in global data transmission. By offering a lower signal loss, reduced maintenance costs, and greater transmission distances, ZBLAN stands to redefine how information is shared worldwide. As the demand for data continues to grow and the infrastructure supporting it struggles to keep pace, ZBLAN fibers could provide a transformative solution, enabling a network that is faster, clearer, and more resilient than ever before. The manufacturing advantages of space are unlocking the full potential of this technology, showing us that the future of global communication may well depend on innovations born in orbit.

The economic potential of ZBLAN fiber optics lies in their ability to vastly outperform traditional silica fibers in data transmission, making them a high-demand product in the telecommunications and data infrastructure sectors. ZBLAN's unique properties—such as lower signal loss and enhanced clarity—address some of the most pressing issues in long-distance data transmission. With global data needs growing exponentially, the demand for reliable, high-capacity infrastructure is skyrocketing. This surge in demand makes ZBLAN fibers, particularly those manufactured in the microgravity of space, a valuable asset with significant commercial potential.

One of the key economic drivers behind space-made ZBLAN is its capacity to reduce signal loss over vast distances, decreasing the need for costly signal repeaters in undersea cables and other long-distance networks. With ZBLAN, data can travel up to 2,000 kilometers before experiencing the level of signal degradation that requires reinforcement in standard silica-based systems. This reduction in infrastructure costs—especially in remote or difficult-to-maintain environments, like ocean floors—translates into substantial savings for telecommunications providers. By limiting the frequency of repeaters, companies can build and maintain networks more cost-effectively, passing the benefits down to consumers in the form of more reliable, faster internet access.

Additionally, ZBLAN's manufacturing in space offers another layer of economic appeal: high-profit margins. Given the challenges and expenses associated with space manufacturing, products produced in orbit must offer significant value to justify their production. ZBLAN fibers meet this requirement, as they can command prices far higher than silica fibers due to their enhanced properties. A single kilogram of ZBLAN fiber could be worth tens of thousands of dollars, and in some cases, estimates suggest it could reach hundreds of thousands in certain applications. The clear economic advantage provided by its superior performance justifies these prices, making it one of the few space-made materials with the immediate potential to yield a return on the investment required for orbital production.

The commercial potential of ZBLAN is further amplified by its application in various fields beyond just data transmission. As more sectors incorporate high-speed, high-clarity data into their operations—from finance and media to healthcare and advanced research—ZBLAN's value extends beyond traditional telecom networks. Medical facilities, for instance, rely heavily on high-speed data for imaging and diagnostics, and ZBLAN's clarity and efficiency could enhance their connectivity and precision. Data centers, which are central to cloud computing and big data, also stand to benefit from ZBLAN's low-loss transmission, enabling faster data processing and storage solutions. This adaptability across industries enhances the market reach of ZBLAN, ensuring a steady demand for its unique capabilities.

In the context of the space economy, ZBLAN fibers represent a tangible opportunity to bring high-value materials back to Earth, a key factor in advancing the commercial case for space manufacturing. The high-profit margins achievable with ZBLAN could offset the costs of space-based production, creating a model that could inspire other materials and products to follow suit. As infrastructure costs in space decrease and the demand for premium data transmission solutions rises, the market potential for ZBLAN fibers will likely expand, solidifying their role as one of the most commercially viable products in the burgeoning space economy.

In essence, the market demand, broad application potential, and high profit margins make ZBLAN an exceptional candidate for space-based manufacturing. Its ability to revolutionize data infrastructure, coupled with its economic viability, positions it as a pioneering product that not only underscores the value of space manufacturing but also drives further interest in the economic possibilities of microgravity production. With ZBLAN, space-made products are no longer speculative investments; they are valuable, high-performing assets that meet real-world needs and generate substantial returns, making them a cornerstone of the next wave in industrial advancement.

# Chapter 6: Building Infrastructure in Space with 3D Printing

The evolution of 3D printing in space has expanded far beyond simple, functional items to encompass complex, mission-critical structures that are advancing the potential of space manufacturing. In its early stages on the International Space Station (ISS), 3D printing was used to create basic tools and replacement parts—objects that could be manufactured on demand, reducing the need for resupply missions and ensuring that astronauts had immediate access to essential items. This initial phase proved the viability of 3D printing in microgravity, demonstrating that even in the absence of Earth's gravity, materials could be layered and fused into usable forms. Since then, the scope of 3D printing has grown dramatically, with new applications and materials emerging that push the boundaries of what can be constructed in space.

As technology has advanced, researchers have turned their focus to printing more sophisticated and larger structures, including infrastructure components, tools, and even experimental habitats. This shift opens up the possibility of constructing elements of spacecraft, satellites, and other support structures directly in orbit, minimizing the need to launch pre-built items from Earth. By creating infrastructure on-site, space missions can reduce launch costs, eliminate payload size restrictions, and adapt more flexibly to mission needs. The eventual goal is to use 3D printing to construct extensive space infrastructure, including large solar arrays, habitat modules, and other elements necessary for sustained human presence in space. This capability would enable a more autonomous approach to space exploration and industry, as these components could be manufactured as needed without relying on Earth-based supply chains.

One of the most promising advancements in space 3D printing is the ability to work with advanced materials that can withstand extreme conditions.

Ceramics, superalloys, and other heat-resistant materials have become focal points in the push to create durable, high-performance structures in space. On Earth, manufacturing items with these materials can be challenging and costly due to their high melting points and the precision required in shaping them. In the controlled environment of microgravity, however, materials solidify more evenly, leading to fewer structural imperfections and stronger, more reliable finished products.

Ceramics, in particular, offer advantages for creating heat-resistant components ideal for the harsh environments encountered in space. For instance, ceramic-based parts could be used in rocket engines, where extreme heat resistance and durability are essential. Ceramics also have applications in thermal shielding, protecting spacecraft from the intense heat of atmospheric re-entry. By 3D printing these components in space, engineers can take advantage of microgravity's ability to produce materials with fewer stress points and more consistent composition, leading to stronger and longer-lasting parts.

Superalloys, another key material in advanced 3D printing, provide exceptional strength and resistance to thermal expansion, making them ideal for structural components exposed to both intense heat and significant mechanical stress. In aerospace applications, superalloys are commonly used in turbine engines and other high-stress environments. Printing these alloys in microgravity can improve their crystalline structure, enhancing their resilience and making them even better suited to demanding applications in space. With this capability, future spacecraft and satellites could incorporate highly resilient parts that endure the stresses of launch, extreme temperature fluctuations, and prolonged exposure to cosmic radiation.

The capacity to work with these advanced materials is pivotal for creating equipment and infrastructure that can support long-term missions, not only around Earth but also for deeper space exploration. With 3D printing, components that would otherwise be difficult to transport or construct on Earth due to size or shape limitations can now be manufactured directly in orbit. This approach reduces the risks and costs associated with launching large or irregularly shaped objects and opens up new possibilities for the construction of resilient space stations, large telescopes, and even potential habitats on the Moon or Mars.

Expanding the scope of 3D printing to include complex structures and advanced materials represents a breakthrough in sustainable space exploration. This technology not only improves mission efficiency by enabling in-situ manufacturing but also enhances the quality and durability of materials used in critical space applications. By combining microgravity's unique effects with innovative materials, 3D printing is leading us toward a future where space infrastructure is robust, adaptable, and capable of supporting human endeavors on an unprecedented scale. As we refine our capabilities with ceramics, superalloys, and other advanced materials, we are moving closer to an era in which constructing entire space habitats, research stations, and power systems directly in orbit will be within our reach.

The Archinaut One project represents a groundbreaking shift in the way we approach constructing satellites and other large structures in space. Developed by Redwire, Archinaut One combines the technologies of 3D printing and robotic assembly to create a new era of self-manufacturing satellites, allowing components to be printed and assembled directly in orbit. This capability overcomes one of the biggest limitations of satellite design: the size and shape constraints imposed by rocket payload fairings. Traditionally, satellites and space infrastructure must be compact enough to fit within the narrow confines of a rocket, requiring complex folding mechanisms and structural compromises to ensure they deploy correctly once in orbit. Archinaut One's technology offers an elegant solution to these challenges, enabling the construction of structures that can be as large and intricate as needed without having to conform to the limitations of an Earth-bound launch.

The vision for Archinaut One is centered around building large solar arrays for satellites directly in space. Solar arrays are essential for powering satellites and space stations, but their efficiency is often limited by the size constraints of Earth-launched designs. With Archinaut One, a satellite can be launched with a basic framework and then construct expansive solar panels in orbit, extending its power-generating capabilities far beyond what would be feasible with traditional launch configurations. This ability to create large solar structures on demand means that even small satellites can enjoy an extended power supply, allowing them to operate for longer periods and support more advanced functions.

The process involves Archinaut One printing components for solar arrays and other structures from raw materials, while robotic arms precisely assemble these components in orbit. Robotic assembly adds a layer of flexibility and precision that further extends the potential applications of this technology. The robotic arms can handle complex tasks that would be difficult or impossible for humans to perform in space, allowing for the construction of structures with intricate designs and configurations tailored to specific mission needs. This approach could be applied to a range of structures, from solar panels to communication arrays, providing greater versatility in satellite and space station design.

In the long term, Archinaut One's capabilities could be expanded to include the construction of massive space structures, such as large antennas, telescopes, and even habitat modules. Without the constraints of gravity or rocket fairings, these structures could be built on a scale that is currently unimaginable for

Earth-bound manufacturing. For example, a telescope with a primary mirror spanning several meters could be printed and assembled in orbit, allowing for unprecedented precision in space observation and opening new avenues for astronomical research. Similarly, the potential to construct habitat modules directly in space brings us closer to the concept of permanent human settlements in orbit, where living spaces can be created and adapted as needed without reliance on Earth-based manufacturing and transport.

The self-manufacturing capabilities of Archinaut One and similar technologies represent a major step toward sustainable space infrastructure. By creating and assembling components in orbit, space missions can become more independent from Earth, reducing the need for costly and complex supply chains. This autonomy is crucial for long-term space exploration goals, such as building a self-sufficient lunar base or supporting Mars missions, where transporting every component from Earth would be logistically challenging and prohibitively expensive.

Beyond exploration, Archinaut One's technology could also support commercial endeavors in space, such as building massive solar power stations that could transmit energy back to Earth. By constructing these power-generating facilities in orbit, energy production could become more efficient and environmentally friendly, harnessing solar energy without the limitations posed by Earth's atmosphere and weather patterns. This concept of space-based solar power stations has been discussed for years, but Archinaut One's technology brings it closer to reality, offering a viable means of creating and maintaining the large infrastructure needed for these systems.

The potential of Archinaut One and robotic assembly in space is transformative. It enables the creation of large, robust structures that not only overcome Earth-bound limitations but also support ambitious projects that could reshape our relationship with space. With the ability to manufacture and assemble directly in orbit, Archinaut One offers a pathway to a future where the construction of infrastructure in space is efficient, adaptable, and sustainable. This technology is setting the foundation for a new era in space exploration and industry, where humanity can build, expand, and thrive beyond our planet with unprecedented freedom and capability.

# Chapter 7: Overcoming Challenges in Space Manufacturing

Space manufacturing and infrastructure projects face a multitude of technical challenges that stem from the unique environment of orbit. One of the most fundamental engineering obstacles is transporting the necessary materials into space. Every kilogram of cargo launched from Earth incurs significant costs, meaning that each piece of equipment and raw material must be meticulously selected and justified. This limitation has prompted engineers to develop lighter, more compact components and explore innovative ways to minimize the amount of material that must be transported. However, until space mining or in-situ resource utilization becomes feasible, transporting supplies from Earth remains a key challenge for space manufacturing projects.

Automation is another critical requirement in space manufacturing, as human presence in orbit is limited and costly. Robotic systems must be capable of performing complex assembly tasks with a high degree of autonomy and precision, as even minor errors could lead to structural failures or render the manufactured components unusable. In the absence of gravity, automation systems must be designed to manage floating materials and maintain control over every aspect of the manufacturing process. Achieving this level of precision is difficult on Earth and even more challenging in space, where microgravity affects the behavior of fluids, solids, and even robotic movements. Advanced robotic arms, sensors, and software are essential to ensuring that automated processes in space can replicate the reliability and accuracy required for long-term success.

Maintaining precision in manufacturing and assembly is equally challenging due to the extreme conditions in space, including temperature fluctuations, radiation exposure, and the constant threat of micrometeoroids. Materials expand and contract in response to these temperature shifts, and equipment must be designed to withstand these stresses while continuing to function with absolute accuracy. Protective measures, such as specialized coatings and resilient materials, must be implemented to guard against radiation and other hazards, adding to the complexity of manufacturing components in space. The need for precision extends to every phase of the process, from the initial printing or construction of parts to their assembly into finished structures. Achieving this level of reliability and durability in orbit remains one of the most pressing technical challenges for space engineers.

Beyond technical issues, space manufacturing also faces significant logistical and economic barriers. Launching equipment and raw materials into orbit is an expensive endeavor, with costs often reaching tens of thousands of dollars per kilogram. This high cost puts substantial pressure on projects to maximize the value of each launch, necessitating careful planning and resource allocation. Limited space aboard rockets also restricts the size and amount of cargo that can be sent, further complicating logistics. Engineers must design compact, modular systems that can be efficiently transported, assembled, and deployed in orbit—a challenging requirement when working with bulky or complex manufacturing equipment.

Another logistical hurdle is the need for a sustainable return on investment (ROI). Space manufacturing projects demand high upfront costs, not only for the launch and equipment but also for ongoing maintenance and operation in orbit. To attract investment and ensure the project's longevity, companies must demonstrate a clear and sustainable path to profitability. For products like ZBLAN fiber optics or bioprinted tissues, the commercial potential exists, but the revenue generated must cover not only the costs of production but also the expenses associated with space transportation and operation. High-value products are essential for making space manufacturing economically viable, as they can justify the investment and help fund future missions.

The economic model for space manufacturing also hinges on creating products that provide distinct advantages over Earth-made alternatives. Investors and stakeholders must be convinced that the added cost of producing in space is offset by superior performance, unique properties, or market demand. For instance, space-made ZBLAN fiber optics offer unparalleled data transmission quality, which can justify their higher price in sectors requiring advanced telecommunications infrastructure. Similarly, bioprinting in microgravity can produce complex tissues with potential applications in regenerative medicine, offering a compelling case for space-based manufacturing. However, these products must reach a scale and market acceptance that can sustain the financial requirements of space operations.

Achieving this balance between cost and value requires innovation, strategic partnerships, and ongoing advancements in technology to reduce expenses associated with space launches and manufacturing. With reusable rockets, new propulsion technologies, and more efficient supply chains, the cost of accessing space may gradually decrease, making the economics of space manufacturing more feasible. Until then, space manufacturing projects must carefully navigate the logistical and economic realities of operating in orbit, balancing ambitious goals with the practicalities of cost, efficiency, and return on investment.

Together, these technical, logistical, and economic barriers underscore the complexity of building a sustainable space manufacturing industry. The challenges are substantial, but with advancements in technology, automation, and production techniques, solutions are gradually emerging that bring the vision of space-based industry closer to reality. Addressing these obstacles is essential to unlocking the full potential of space manufacturing, allowing humanity to expand its capabilities beyond Earth and build an infrastructure that supports not only exploration but also economic growth and innovation in orbit.

Solutions are emerging that could address some of the steep costs and technical hurdles currently facing space manufacturing. One of the most promising developments on the horizon is the advancement of infrastructure to support more affordable and efficient space operations. Larger rockets and reusable spacecraft are key to reducing launch costs, a fundamental barrier to expanding space-based industry. Reusable rockets, pioneered by companies like SpaceX, represent a paradigm shift by drastically lowering the expense of sending materials and equipment into orbit. Each rocket that can be reused multiple times reduces the need to build new launch vehicles, saving millions per launch. Over time, the economic advantages of reusable spacecraft will compound, making routine space travel more financially feasible and allowing for regular, cost-effective missions to resupply and support space manufacturing facilities.

Larger rockets also play a vital role in enabling the construction of more extensive infrastructure in space. Rockets with higher payload capacities can carry bigger, heavier loads, which means that more substantial equipment and supplies can be transported in fewer trips. This capability allows for the transport of complete modules, large-scale manufacturing equipment, and even prefabricated components for in-orbit assembly. SpaceX's Starship, for instance, is designed to carry significantly larger payloads than previous rockets, providing the capacity needed to support ambitious projects like Orbital Reef or in-space factories. With this expanded cargo space, manufacturers can plan larger projects without being as limited by rocket dimensions, opening up new possibilities for infrastructure and production in orbit.

The role of government and the private sector is crucial in making these advancements feasible and accelerating progress in space manufacturing. Government agencies such as NASA, ESA, and others have historically led the way in space exploration and technological development, creating a foundation upon which the commercial space sector is now building. Policies that encourage collaboration between public agencies and private companies are instrumental in advancing space infrastructure. For instance, NASA's partnerships with SpaceX and Blue Origin have allowed these companies to develop new technologies with the benefit of government expertise and funding, resulting in innovations that are now helping reduce the cost and complexity of space travel.

Public funding plays a vital role in de-risking the development of new technologies and infrastructure. Government investment in space programs and infrastructure projects helps establish a stable environment where private companies can test and refine their technologies without bearing the entire financial risk. Programs such as NASA's Commercial Crew and Commercial Resupply Services demonstrate how public funding can foster innovation, enabling private companies to develop reusable rockets, automated systems, and other crucial technologies. These partnerships lower costs, improve reliability, and create a knowledge base that benefits the entire industry, accelerating progress toward sustainable space manufacturing.

Private investment is also essential for driving the commercial viability of space manufacturing. Venture capital and corporate investment provide the funding needed for research, development, and scaling production capabilities. Unlike public funding, which is often directed toward foundational infrastructure and technology, private investment tends to focus on products with clear market potential, such as ZBLAN fiber optics, bioprinted tissues, or advanced manufacturing systems. The influx of private capital incentivizes companies to innovate rapidly and focus on developing products that offer immediate commercial value, helping space manufacturing move from concept to profitable reality.

Governments also play a role in crafting policies and regulations that support a sustainable space industry. For example, policies related to orbital resource rights, safety protocols, and space debris management are critical for ensuring that space remains a viable environment for commercial activity. Clear guidelines on the ownership and usage of space resources could encourage more companies to invest in space manufacturing by providing legal clarity and reducing uncertainty. International cooperation, led by government agencies, can also help address global issues such as space traffic management and the mitigation of space debris, both of which are essential for maintaining safe and sustainable operations in orbit.

Ultimately, the combined efforts of public funding, private investment, and supportive government policies are creating a framework that will make space manufacturing a feasible, sustainable industry. As infrastructure improvements like larger rockets and reusable spacecraft continue to reduce costs, and as policies evolve to support commercial space activities, the vision of an economy beyond Earth grows closer to reality. This collaborative model is transforming space from a field of exploration into an arena of economic activity, where innovation thrives, and new industries emerge. By addressing the practical and economic challenges of operating in orbit, these solutions are laying the groundwork for a future where humanity can harness the resources and opportunities of space, making it an integral part of our economic landscape.

# Chapter 8: Environmental and Ethical Considerations

Sustainability in space is a critical consideration as humanity embarks on an era of increased orbital activity and the growth of space-based industries. Effective waste management, responsible resource usage, and a strategic approach to reducing environmental impacts are essential to ensuring that this new frontier remains viable and beneficial in the long term. With the potential for space manufacturing, bioprinting, and large-scale infrastructure projects on the horizon, careful planning is required to manage waste and protect both Earth's orbit and the broader space environment.

Waste management in space is uniquely challenging due to the lack of natural disposal mechanisms and the potential dangers posed by debris. Even small fragments of waste or discarded equipment can become dangerous projectiles in orbit, capable of causing significant damage to satellites, spacecraft, or manufacturing facilities. To address this, companies and space agencies are exploring methods for safely disposing of waste in orbit or returning it to Earth. Some approaches include compacting and securely storing waste until it can be removed, recycling materials within the space manufacturing process, or creating "reusable" modules that can be adapted and repurposed rather than discarded. By minimizing waste and promoting closed-loop systems, space operations can reduce their environmental footprint and mitigate the risks associated with orbital debris.

Resource usage in space is another essential factor for sustainability. Transporting resources from Earth is both costly and environmentally taxing, so there is a strong incentive to use materials efficiently and to consider in-situ resource utilization (ISRU) for future projects. ISRU involves harvesting resources from space environments, such as mining water from the Moon or asteroids, to support space-based operations. Water, for instance, could be used for life support, radiation shielding, or even fuel production. In the longer term, ISRU could reduce the demand for Earth-based resources, making space manufacturing less dependent on Earth's supply chains and more sustainable overall.

One of the most promising aspects of space manufacturing lies in its potential environmental benefits for Earth. By relocating certain high-pollution industries to orbit, humanity could reduce some of the environmental stress on our planet. Traditional manufacturing, especially for high-tech products, often involves processes that generate pollutants and greenhouse gases. Producing items like fiber optics, semiconductors, or even certain metals in space could eliminate some of these emissions, as space factories could operate without directly impacting Earth's air, water, or soil.

The unique properties of microgravity also offer a more sustainable method of production for some materials. For instance, ZBLAN fiber optics and certain pharmaceuticals can be manufactured with higher efficiency and fewer defects in space, reducing waste compared to Earth-based production. By producing these high-value products in orbit, companies could achieve greater resource efficiency, meaning fewer raw materials are wasted in the production process. In this way, space-based manufacturing could help curb Earth's resource consumption and pollution footprint, especially for products that require energy-intensive processes or toxic chemicals.

Moreover, the long-term vision of building solar power stations in space offers a significant environmental benefit for Earth. Space-based solar arrays could capture sunlight without interference from the atmosphere or clouds, providing a continuous and highly efficient source of renewable energy. This energy could potentially be transmitted to Earth via microwaves or lasers, providing clean energy with minimal environmental impact. Such a shift could reduce the need for fossil fuel power plants and lower global carbon emissions, contributing to climate change mitigation efforts.

While space manufacturing and infrastructure development carry their own environmental risks, a sustainable approach could yield substantial benefits for both space and Earth. By adopting responsible waste management practices, optimizing resource use, and leveraging space's unique environment to reduce pollution, humanity can ensure that the expansion into space supports ecological goals rather than compromising them. As we develop the infrastructure to support a thriving space economy, sustainability will be crucial to balancing growth with the protection of both Earth's environment and the delicate ecosystems of space. In this way, space activities have the potential not only to preserve Earth's environment but also to contribute actively to a cleaner, more sustainable future.

As space becomes a commercial domain, ethical considerations surrounding access, ownership, and the equitable distribution of benefits become increasingly significant. The question of who has the right to exploit resources, conduct research, or establish operations in orbit or beyond is central to these discussions. Space, once the domain of national exploration and scientific collaboration, is now an arena where private enterprises and governments are vying for opportunities and profits. This shift toward commercialization raises ethical questions about ownership, fairness, and how to ensure that the vast potential of space benefits all of humanity rather than a select few.

One key ethical concern is the distribution of benefits derived from space activities. Private companies like SpaceX, Blue Origin, and Redwire, which are pioneering advancements in space manufacturing, resource extraction, and satellite infrastructure, are positioned to reap substantial economic rewards. However, the benefits generated by these activities could become concentrated among a small number of companies and their shareholders, potentially deepening economic disparities. The profits and technological advancements gained from space could remain inaccessible to those without the resources to participate in space ventures, leading to a scenario where the commercial opportunities of space reinforce existing inequalities.

Access to space is another critical ethical issue. Space remains highly exclusive due to the immense costs associated with reaching and operating in orbit, which limits participation to wealthy nations and corporations. As private companies and affluent individuals secure their place in space, the ability of smaller nations or organizations to access and benefit from space technology could diminish. This exclusivity risks creating a divide between those who can access and utilize space for economic or scientific purposes and those who cannot, raising questions about fairness and the equitable distribution of opportunities.

Resource extraction from celestial bodies, such as asteroids or the Moon, also presents ethical challenges. These resources, while technically available to all humanity under international treaties like the Outer Space Treaty of 1967, could soon become the focus of intense competition. Private companies and a few well-funded countries may begin mining these resources, raising questions about who truly "owns" space resources and whether their extraction should be regulated. The Outer Space Treaty stipulates that space is the "province of all mankind," meaning that its resources should benefit all people, not just those with the means to access them. However, current regulatory frameworks are limited, and as space mining becomes feasible, new policies will be required to address ownership, environmental concerns, and fair distribution.

These ethical questions bring to light the need for a robust international framework that addresses commercial activities in space. Developing policies that ensure space remains a shared domain, with fair access and benefits for all, is essential. An effective approach might involve creating a global space regulatory body that oversees resource usage, environmental protections, and equitable access. This organization could establish guidelines to prevent monopolization of space resources, ensure transparency in commercial operations, and create mechanisms for less-advantaged nations to benefit from space-related advancements. For instance, companies engaged in space mining could contribute a percentage of their profits to a global fund dedicated to supporting scientific research or technology access for developing countries, fostering a more inclusive approach to space's opportunities.

There is also a need for ethical guidelines regarding environmental protection in space. The potential for over-exploitation of space resources, the creation of space debris, and the environmental impact on celestial bodies raises moral concerns about humanity's stewardship of space. Policies that promote responsible exploration and limit environmental damage could help preserve space as a viable domain for future generations. As companies and nations expand their reach beyond Earth, they must consider not only their immediate gains but also their long-term impact on space ecosystems and the preservation of the orbital environment.

Addressing these ethical implications requires global collaboration and a commitment to ensuring that space activities align with humanity's broader values of fairness, environmental stewardship, and shared progress. As space becomes an extension of human enterprise, it must reflect our aspirations for equity and sustainability, rather than reinforcing existing inequalities. A well-governed approach to space commercialization can help to ensure that the benefits of this new frontier are accessible to all, preserving space as a common heritage that inspires and uplifts humanity as a whole.

# Chapter 9: The Future of Space Manufacturing

Over the next decade, space manufacturing is poised to evolve from its current experimental phase into a more mature and integrated industry, driven by advances in technology and infrastructure. As reusable rockets, larger payload capacities, and automated assembly systems become more refined, the economic and logistical barriers that currently hinder space-based production will begin to diminish. This evolution will open up new possibilities for manufacturing in microgravity, where the unique conditions allow for high-quality production of specialized materials, such as advanced fiber optics, pharmaceuticals, and bioprinted tissues, which are challenging or costly to make on Earth. With these advancements, space could become a strategic site for producing goods that address real-world demands, ultimately reshaping key sectors within the global economy.

The first phase of this evolution will likely see space manufacturing facilities expanding their capabilities, moving from small-scale experimental setups to more extensive, autonomous production units capable of creating complex products on demand. Projects like Orbital Reef and Archinaut One are laying the groundwork for this transition by providing flexible platforms for manufacturing, research, and assembly in orbit. Within the next decade, we may see specialized modules dedicated to producing high-value goods with consistent quality, from super-clear ZBLAN fiber optics to advanced alloys and ceramics that exceed Earth-made equivalents. As infrastructure like these modular space stations grows, the consistency and efficiency of space-based production will also improve, making it a more attractive option for industries on Earth.

One of the most transformative aspects of this shift will be the gradual integration of space-produced materials into Earth's economy. The unique properties of items manufactured in microgravity open up applications across various industries, where they can provide advantages over traditionally manufactured products. For instance, ZBLAN fiber optics, produced in space to avoid crystallization defects, could become the new standard in telecommunications, allowing for faster and more reliable data transmission with reduced signal loss. This breakthrough alone could transform the way global data infrastructure is developed, reducing the need for signal repeaters in undersea cables and lowering the costs associated with long-distance data transmission. Telecommunications companies could benefit from lower maintenance costs and improved service quality, while consumers could experience faster and more stable internet connections, even in remote locations.

In the pharmaceutical and healthcare industries, space-produced items like bioprinted tissues and stem cells hold the potential to change how we approach regenerative medicine and drug testing. Tissues and organs printed in microgravity could one day be used in transplants, offering a solution to organ shortages and reducing complications related to immune rejection. The ability to print tissues with more natural structural integrity could also accelerate drug testing, allowing pharmaceutical companies to trial medications on human-like tissues, speeding up the development of safe and effective treatments. As these medical applications move from experimental phases to practical applications, they could reduce healthcare costs, improve patient outcomes, and spur innovation in regenerative therapies.

The integration of space manufacturing into Earth's economy also offers benefits for industries requiring advanced materials, such as aerospace, defense, and electronics. Superalloys and ceramics produced in orbit, which have fewer defects and higher strength than their Earth-made counterparts, could be used to create lighter, more durable components for aircraft, spacecraft, and military equipment. Electronics companies could leverage space-manufactured materials for the production of components with increased resilience and thermal stability, leading to more powerful, long-lasting devices. These materials could find further applications in clean energy, supporting the development of heat-resistant materials for solar panels and wind turbines, enhancing the efficiency and sustainability of energy production on Earth.

The economic potential of space-manufactured goods will likely drive demand for even greater infrastructure and investment in space, creating a feedback loop that further strengthens the industry. As costs decrease with improved space access and reusable technology, more companies may begin exploring the benefits of space production, leading to an expanded market for space-made products. The entry of new players could drive innovation, competition, and cost reductions, making space manufacturing accessible not only to large corporations but potentially to smaller companies and research institutions. This democratization of space manufacturing could further accelerate technological progress, creating a dynamic space economy that complements and enhances Earth-based industries.

Looking forward, space manufacturing could become an essential pillar of Earth's economy, contributing to sustainable growth and reducing the environmental impact of certain industries. As manufacturing moves off-planet, industries traditionally associated with pollution, such as mining or chemical processing, could relocate some operations to space, alleviating strain on Earth's ecosystems. This shift could contribute to cleaner air, water, and soil on Earth while preserving resources for future generations. At the same time, space manufacturing offers a path to sustainable growth that capitalizes on the vast resources and unique conditions available in space.

In the coming decade, space manufacturing stands to become a crucial part of humanity's industrial landscape, forging connections between space and Earth that transcend exploration alone. By integrating space-produced materials into mainstream markets, this industry could reshape telecommunications, healthcare, electronics, and other sectors, driving economic growth while advancing technological capabilities. As the boundaries between Earth and space continue to blur, space manufacturing is poised to be not just an off-world curiosity but a transformative force in creating a sustainable and prosperous future for all.

The long-term vision for space manufacturing extends beyond Earth's orbit, encompassing the Moon, Mars, and other celestial bodies as potential sites for industry and production. While manufacturing in low Earth orbit (LEO) has opened new possibilities, moving beyond Earth's orbit could bring an even greater range of resources, unique environmental benefits, and strategic advantages. With technological advancements in infrastructure, automation, and resource utilization, the Moon and Mars could serve as industrial hubs, supporting everything from sustainable exploration to interplanetary economic growth.

The Moon is an ideal candidate for the next phase of off-Earth manufacturing. As Earth's closest celestial neighbor, the Moon offers relatively easy access compared to other planets or asteroids, requiring lower energy and shorter travel times for missions. Lunar manufacturing could capitalize on abundant in-situ resources, such as lunar regolith, which contains valuable minerals like silicon, aluminum, and iron, all of which are essential for construction and electronics. Using local materials could significantly reduce the need to transport raw supplies from Earth, lowering costs and enabling the construction of large-scale infrastructure directly on the Moon's surface. This infrastructure could include research facilities, energy production stations, and habitats that support ongoing exploration.

One promising application of lunar resources is the production of solar power stations on the Moon. With its lack of atmosphere and near-constant exposure to sunlight at certain polar regions, the Moon offers ideal conditions for harvesting solar energy. Large solar arrays could be built using locally mined materials and assembled using automated robotic systems, providing a continuous and powerful energy source. This energy could be used to power lunar operations, or, with further technological advancements, it might be beamed back to Earth as a clean energy source, creating a sustainable cycle of energy production that supports both Earth and lunar activities.

Manufacturing on Mars presents additional challenges but also vast potential for long-term human settlement and industrial expansion. Mars is rich in minerals and contains water ice, which is essential for both life support and the production of rocket fuel through the electrolysis of water into hydrogen and oxygen. With an autonomous manufacturing base on Mars, it would become possible to produce essential materials for habitat construction, equipment repair, and fuel generation. This capability would enable self-sustaining colonies on Mars, where supplies could be produced locally rather than relying on costly resupply missions from Earth. Mars' weaker gravity (about one-third of Earth's) and thin atmosphere also reduce some of the challenges of launching manufactured goods from its surface, which could facilitate the movement of Martian products to other locations in the solar system.

For Mars manufacturing to be viable, robotic and autonomous systems will need to advance further, given the challenges of remote operations and the time delay in communication with Earth. Automated mining, processing, and assembly robots would be essential to establishing a productive base on Mars before human settlers arrive. Once established, a manufacturing facility on Mars could support the development of a true interplanetary economy, producing resources and products that benefit colonies and missions across the solar system. As Mars manufacturing scales, it could even become a launching point for deep space exploration, providing a hub where spacecraft can be refueled and outfitted for missions to the asteroid belt or beyond.

Asteroids also represent a long-term opportunity for manufacturing and resource extraction. Rich in metals such as platinum, nickel, and iron, certain asteroids contain rare elements that are valuable for high-tech industries and essential for creating sustainable infrastructure in space. Robotic mining missions could extract these resources, refining them in orbit or transporting them to facilities on the Moon or Mars for further processing. Asteroid resources could help reduce humanity's reliance on Earth's finite supply of rare metals, supporting the production of advanced electronics, renewable energy systems, and aerospace technologies both in space and on Earth.

The potential for beyond-Earth manufacturing extends even further to concepts like space habitats and solar power stations that could orbit various planets or moons. By manufacturing these structures in space, without the constraints of Earth's gravity or atmospheric interference, humanity could construct massive facilities that support long-term habitation, resource production, and energy generation. Imagine a network of manufacturing bases and habitats stretching across the solar system, linked by transport routes and powered by solar energy. This network would allow for a level of human mobility, economic expansion, and resilience that is currently only the realm of science fiction.

The long-term vision for manufacturing beyond Earth's orbit is one of resilience, autonomy, and sustainability. By utilizing local resources, leveraging automation, and building robust infrastructures on the Moon, Mars, and beyond, humanity can reduce its dependency on Earth-based supplies and create a more sustainable presence in space. This approach not only supports exploration and settlement but also lays the foundation for an interplanetary economy that could transform how we use resources, produce energy, and expand human civilization. Through manufacturing on the Moon, Mars, and even asteroids, we are inching closer to a future where space is not just a destination but a dynamic environment where human ingenuity, industry, and collaboration can thrive.

## Conclusion

As humanity stands at the brink of a new frontier, the potential and transformative power of space manufacturing is becoming increasingly clear. What began as experimental research and pioneering efforts in low Earth orbit has rapidly evolved into an industry with far-reaching implications for technology, healthcare, infrastructure, and even our relationship with the natural world. Space manufacturing offers unprecedented opportunities to produce materials of superior quality, advance medicine through bioprinting and regenerative therapies, and create sustainable, high-performance infrastructure that Earth's environment simply cannot support. Through the unique environment of microgravity, space manufacturing is revealing possibilities that go beyond solving Earth-based challenges—it is showing us a pathway toward entirely new ways of living, working, and creating.

The journey toward a thriving space economy is still in its early stages, but the vision of manufacturing on the Moon, Mars, and beyond is no longer a distant dream. With advancements in reusable rockets, autonomous systems, and the development of infrastructure like Orbital Reef and Archinaut One, we are moving closer to a reality where space becomes an extension of Earth's economy. This new industrial domain is poised to reshape global markets, foster scientific breakthroughs, and even alleviate some of the environmental pressures on our planet by relocating resource-intensive processes to orbit. Space manufacturing stands to not only benefit those directly involved in its ventures but also provide broader benefits for humanity, from improved telecommunications to cleaner energy and revolutionary medical treatments.

As we look toward this emerging era, it's important to consider how these developments might impact everyday life and drive global progress. Space manufacturing has the potential to make advanced technologies and resources accessible to all, bridging gaps in connectivity, healthcare, and industry that currently hinder economic growth and quality of life for millions. The progress we make in space could help us tackle some of Earth's most pressing issues, inspiring innovation, creating jobs, and fostering a sense of global collaboration as we work to build a future that includes all of humanity. This new era asks us to imagine a world where space is not just a destination for a few but a shared domain that enhances the lives of people everywhere.

As we stand on the threshold of this exciting frontier, let us embrace the unknown with curiosity and determination. The story of space manufacturing is not only a tale of scientific and technological achievement but also a testament to human resilience, creativity, and the relentless pursuit of knowledge. As we push the boundaries of what is possible, we are not only expanding our horizons in a physical sense but also reshaping our understanding of who we are and what we can accomplish together. The journey into space is, at its heart, a journey into the future—one where humanity's ingenuity, courage, and vision will light the way to boundless opportunities.

Let this be an invitation to think beyond our current limits and to see space manufacturing as a crucial part of our shared future. The possibilities are immense, the challenges are great, and the rewards promise to redefine what it means to thrive as a civilization. As we move forward, let's carry with us a sense of excitement and wonder for what lies ahead, inspired by the knowledge that we are only at the beginning of a new era, one that holds potential far beyond what we can yet imagine. Together, we are stepping into a future where the stars are not just lights in the sky but the foundations of the next chapter of human progress.

www.ingramcontent.com/pod-product-compliance
Lightning Source LLC
Chambersburg PA
CBHW070244220526
45465CB00004B/1512